Ink on Snow

Elizabeth Raby

VIRTUAL ARTISTS COLLECTIVE
http://vacpoetry.org
ISBN: 978-0-9819898-4-6

"Cetate (Fortress) Deva, Romania" appeared in slightly different form in the Harwood Arts Center Anthology, Looking Back to Place, Harwood's Old School Books, 2008. "Dream," "The Order of Things," "My Savanna," and "January" appeared in Camphorwood, Nightshade Press, 1992. "In Transit" appeared in Ten Degrees above Zero, Jasper Press, 2005. "The Ship is Sinking, He Said," "True Dark," "A woman's secret name," and "Moving toward infinity in these meandering transient details" were translated into Romanian by Casandra Ioan and appeared in Discobolul, Alba Iulia, Romania in the May, June, July, 2009 issue. "Bride-to-Be" was the winning poem, 2010 Kelton Poetry Contest, sponsored by Angelo State University Writer's Conference and Concho River Review where it will appear in the Autumn 2010 issue. "At the Door" will appear in U.S. 1 Worksheets. "Lake Champlain" appeared in Vol. 53, 2008, and "Lost Stories" in Vol. 54, 2009. "Women Writing" appeared as "Young Women Writing Poems" in Central Avenue, Vol.5, Issue 9, August 2007. "Flashes" was in Mad Poets Review, Vol. 21, and "The October Patio" in Vol. 22. "Prayer" will appear in The Comstock Review, Vol. 23, No. 2. "Russian Olive" appeared in Texas Poetry Calendar 2009 and "At the Wheel of the Year" appeared in Texas Poetry Calendar 2010. "Living on Earth" appeared in The Enigmatist, December 2009.

With gratitude to Steven Schroeder, to Regina Schroeder, to Christopher Bursk, to Judyth Hill's and Rachelle Woods' inspirational gatherings of poets, to the Eldorado writing group, and to Sou Vai Keng.

For Patricia Goodrich whose energy, generosity, and spirit of adventure have brought so many good things into my life, and for Jim Raby, my dear partner and one-man booster club.

Table of Contents

The Veiled Woman

The gate between worlds
is unlatched. Then winter
hammers the chains that keep
the Veiled Woman, a dried
brown husk, a closed seed,
underground. In her darkness
she waits to be broken, spilled,
released, to return as she has
always done when light
softens and unseals her.

I

Cetate (Fortress) Deva, Romania

A small stone monument stands
behind an iron gate beneath curved brick
of the otherwise empty dungeon.
Here David Ferenc the founder
of the Unitarian Church was martyred
in the prison of this castle, 1579

Outside, the courtyard is littered
with bits of stone, ragweed, plastic,
cigarette butts, crumbling bricks.
A painted blue peace sign fades
on gray stone, names are scratched
on broken walls.

Something white protrudes from packed
earth. She picks it up before she recognizes
a tooth, the enamel perfect, the root unscarred,
wrenched from some young human mouth.

All around the exhalation of souls
slips past in the air above her, touches
her skin, gently entreats her to know them,
to ask what happened here and why.

The atoms of the anonymous mingle
with those who kept them so, who wanted
them to remain polite in their graves, in their
blowing ash, their stories and their anguish
lost. Still they whisper and nudge, a quiet
disturbance of the atmosphere.

In Sighişoara, Romania

The artist sets up her paintings,
sits in the sunshine on a broken stone
at a corner of the house
where Vlad lived as a little boy,
before his father lent him
to the sultan as hostage, before
the beatings, before he saw what
torture was, before he watched
the slicings and slittings, learned
how it was done, before he grew up,
came home, became Vlad Ţepeş,
the Impaler, invited the sultan
to dinner, greeted him with the sight
of 20,000 soldiers, the sultan's best,
skewered and staked-up in the garden,
before even the sultan gagged, went home.

But today it is all so long ago,
Vlad still a hero to this town,
even un-mourned Ceaşuescu
dead twenty years. The artist
is free to paint as she pleases.
What pleases are tiny landscapes
of shady lanes, fields of daisies
beneath summer skies. Her
little daughter has set up her own
easel, offers her water-color
round-faced girls in bright
dresses, surrounded by flowers,
as though the girls too were
growing cheerful petals,
red, blue, gold, in this young
artist's good and bounteous garden.

On the Train from Deva to Budapest

One old, her yellow blouse
held
by straining buttons,
one young,
a white polo shirt
over new breasts—
two gypsies,
pleated spangled skirts
brushing
the compartment's
filthy floor,
an occasional glimpse
of gold teeth,
a strand of dark hair
escaping
a burgundy and gold
flowered scarf.

The girl's tentative smile,
offer to share her sandwich,
a giggling lesson
in Romanian,
a proffered cell phone number,
an invitation to visit
anytime,
a moment
without history
in a world
of nothing but.

Dream

First comes the awful roar,
fills our head, overwhelms the house.

We run outside—
sounds crowd the sky.

There are three of them flying
in close formation,
enormous, khaki-plated.

Dread swells with the noise
and the blue-green light
angled down from their undersides.

What they pass over appears undamaged
but they do damage.
They leave behind
ghost trees, ghost houses, ghost people.
Now they are over us...

Yield

In the universe's vast memory
somewhere families huddle
telling the first stories.
Into their beating hearts,
through the souls of their feet,
they absorb the contradictions
that shape and shadow our lives.
From language to revision—
a spear, a needle, a sinew, collected
seeds, water brought in woven baskets,
charms and signs to put them first,
to keep them fed and safe. They have
not yet heard that ice both advances
and retreats, or of violent impacts,
eruptions, slow convulsive slide and
smash of continents, birth and death
of stars, final inexorable drift
of galaxies ever outward and apart.

A World Where

The spirits of children gradually broken
In white cribs in blank rooms,
In burning huts of swords and terror,
In a continual abrasion of promises not kept.

The spirits of children that survive
The hole blown in the bake shop,
The long walk past everything gone,
The uncle's inappropriate hands.

Babies replete in warm flannel,
Babies who cry at shriveled breasts.
Children who play happily in courtyards of dust.
Children discontent beneath a toy hill of plastic.

For the first time in months a girl smiles, her mother
gone to prison, a heavy weight removed.

Frieda's Table

Set with snowy linen,
pickle dishes, relish cups,
plates ready for herring
and beets, crystal goblets,
white embroidered napkins,
starched until, folded, they
stood at crisp attention
on white china, its basket-
weave borders rimmed in gold.

Friends are joining us
for dinner—she often said
on a Friday as she led me
to her basement massage table—
I need to be prepared
before sundown.

There in the almost dark
for one delicious hour,
she oiled, kneaded, flexed,
tapped my body as she
spoke softly of her life
in the camps, how young
she had been, her husband
taken away, her guilt at not
having loved him, how she lost
her mother, father, sister,
cousins, uncles, aunts.

How, after the war in a DP camp
she met Richard, his wife
and baby daughter gone. He
was undone in grief. Frieda
brought him slowly back to life.

How they found their way
to Pennsylvania and a surviving
relative or two, how they prospered
until they lost their little store,
how Richard's heart was too bad
for work now, how they made do
with what Frieda earned.

At the end of the hour she
always kissed me. I wondered
that she could stand the feel
of human flesh. She stopped
to inspect her table, shifted
a goblet an inch to the left,
let me find my own way out.

Contact

The orangutan is first to reach out,
proffer a cluster of leaves
to the man who studies him
from a rope perch fixed high
in the rainforest canopy.
The man, surprised by the gift,
soon understands—the effort
requires a gesture in return.
He extends a leafy branch
to the waiting ape who tastes it
carefully. Then from the end
of a long hairy red arm,
tentative black fingers unfold
across the gap. The man
stretches out his own
cautious hand. For an instant
their fingers touch.
As innocent as Adam,
the young creature does not
know of the expulsion
that often comes next.

The Order of Things

We gather in soft light
under the civilized joke
of cherubs and clouds
painted on the ceiling
of this revolutionary-era
stone house that leans
over the canal. We share
plates of fleshy peppers,
red, gold, yellow,
grilled Italian-style
over charcoal. Relaxed
we exchange stories.

She tells us her dream.
An underwater cave—
up from enfolded beds
of seaweed and coral,
past sinuous wings
and whips of rays,
motion of squid and fish,
she is forced through
green slime, sea grass,
onto a shore of jumbled rock.

For a moment the world
becomes a film inserted
backwards: secret poisons
left on the peppers, people
I see through the window
gathered under the bridge,
fire in their trash can,
the beginning of our evolution,

not the end. In some cosmic
reversal, I weep on the wrong
side of the womb.

Incoming

In the huddle of your family,
in the scent of unwashed hair,
unwashed clothes, you rub
your fingers over the little hand
in yours, feel ragged thumbnail,
torn cuticle, listen to the baby's
steady sobs, press your cheek
against your husband's clenched
furious back, close your eyes
and pray for an end to explosions,
bursts of white phosphorous,
screams of people and sirens.

You bargain—you don't ask
for food, or water, or cooking gas.
You would even forgo forever
the feel of your children's bodies,
soaped, rinsed, wrapped in towels,
held close to your chest,
sweetness of calm hearts
beating against yours, if only...

Just this one little thing—a scrap
of roof, enough standing wall,
a corner to keep them safe.

Dreaming Anomalies

Last night in sleep
I saw pink cabbage roses
painted across pale green silk,
a man drawing hand-sized
pansies on heavy paper
in thick purple and gold.

Once as Grandmother delivered
flower-filled May baskets
by horse and buggy, lightning struck,
burnt her home to ash behind her.
Grandmother's first and only
silk dress, spinach green damask,
tiny tucks, a white lace collar, was gone
before she ever wore it. She
dreamed of it forever.

Once they have seen them,
perhaps all women dream
of flowers and silk—
Chinese prisoners who worked
the looms; girls who cut
parachutes away from dead pilots
and saved the silk to fashion dresses
despite the red blood
that bloomed across it.

In Transit

A stranger here, the visitor walks
alone on quiet streets restored to brick
and gingerbread perfection. There

a sign points to a wooden stable,
a stop on the Underground Railway,
its shuttered slits of windows and

faded blue-green paint diminished
beneath a grove of mammoth trees.
The stable must have looked like this then,

the anxious sweat and throb
of runaways, willing to risk their last
anonymous breath, concealed inside.

Hard by, brush-covered banks drop
to a creek, a shallow waterway
that hid scents of fear and hope

from men and dogs who stalked
the freedom road. Behind these
neighboring doors, neat curtains,

some knew, helped, did nothing, betrayed.
The stranger wonders what would she
have done. What does she do now?

Disequilibrium

What does it mean?
     this heavy wind from the south

Where will we find water?
     when fires run down resiny slopes

The coyote stops at the stone basin
     outside the window
     for a solitary drink

Last year when rains were plentiful
     there was first a pair and then a pack
     now alone she continues on her obdurate way

The Ship is Sinking, He Said

At the harbor a phone rang and she
was frightened. Brown fog rose into a yellow sky.

Headlights swept rain-soaked streets. What is that
pile of rages?

We must choose a different restaurant. This spoils
one's dinner. Even the pink cloth, soft candlelight,
odor of lamb and red wine don't hide the stink at the door.

There once were wolves here. They followed
the bison. There is no room for either now.

No, John, no news tonight. A warm bath, a soft robe,
and then a little music.

How long since we looked out that window?
It must be years since we swam in the lake,
felt rain on our already wet faces.

Do you hear that? It sounds like tramping feet.
Can that be a siren? The night is so pleasant,
the golden hammock of the moon so bright.
This is a peaceful street.

Oh, milk of lost mornings.
Oh, black metal night.

II

Bride-to-Be

Walking alone as she likes best,
beside dried mullein, its seed heads
open, old burrs bent double by the weight
of snow, she is startled by a dead root
reclining like a body with legs spread,
one knee bent, crack of vagina, chest
open, heart torn out, a single staring eye.
There one ant, more vigorous than she
will ever be, searches the small debris
of pine needles, tiny twigs, bits of dirt,
fallen into the broken wood.

She watches stellar jays, blue as the glass rods
that curtained the Temple of Heaven,
move in courtship climb up sun-spackled
vanilla-scented ponderosa pine. A pair
of tiny bushtits touch beaks on a slender
branch above juicy new sedum, spikes
of chive in bud. Here in brisk welcome
every dead stalk is fringed in green.

She begins a long climb past red
shoots of peonies, birches leaking sap,
until she reaches the peak at last.
Sunset colors melting snow violet red.
For now, she is replete, but tomorrow
she will leave behind these solitary
explorations, everything she knows.
She doesn't want to be opened and split,
a character in a man's life: She is afraid
to be tugged out of herself by a child.
If she could just remain here watching
geese fly toward the waxing moon.

Stellar Jay

What does the jay see
when he sees me?
What does he know
or care to know?
Is my lack of a black crest,
white spots
above a beak,
feathers
like lapis lazuli
a matter of concern?

If his brain
were a bit
bigger, I could
love him,
his raucous voice,
glorious ability
to soar
above the world,
beauties of feather
and flight. I could
imagine him
my size,
hide beneath his blue
and sheltering wing.

True Dark

If there weren't light,

only fields hidden in darkness,

eyes without luminescence,

black seas, a coal of sky,

the weight of night without

the piquancy of stars,

the moon's pale throat—

There is no one

I have loved enough

to be the light for me—

whose absence would make

the world forever dark

Unrest

Will nothing satisfy me?
I walk in the field, solid
with autumn flowers. When
winter comes, their stems will
crack, and brown flower-heads
lie down under the snow:
each flower un-resistant
to the order of its days.
Now, outside the window dark
descends. A black outline
of trees moves in the wind.
I am in a room within a room.
I arrange goldenrod, white
yarrow, the vague licorice
of purple hyssop, stalks
of Artemisia. I crush silver
knots of bloom. Spice fills
my hands. All day I've
wanted you, your voice,
to intensify and shape
                    this silence.

My Savanna

up black rivers
the source
in tangled whorls of damp
night meadow
small nests
hummocks of your chest
the grassland of your beard
a flock of dark
swallows around your head

To Be Here

For Jim

Still so cold, this moment
before spring.

What change signifies the wind
roaring through the trees
apparently in four directions?

Whether it means bad weather
or an imminent turn to melt
and warmth, I will not inquire.

Whatever it foretells, I am glad
to be here to feel it, to know,
this year at least, I still have you.

Masquerades

I.

He unfolded webbed fingers,
  extended giant forearms,
for a moment I thought I could
  see through the veined membranes
as they spread wide against the light,
  but once again folding wings
pulled me against dark implacable fur.
  It is what I knew best.

II.

If I could have sheltered you
in my body shielded you

if your brain could have entered
my brain if I could have felt
its vast and intricate firings
its flashes

if I could have fed
your strength you mine
the serpent swallowing itself

A woman's secret name—

Everyday she swallows it,
chokes it back. Her throat
swells with the effort.

It lurks there just
beyond her uttering,
their hearing.

She will give it up
to no one. It weaves its way
through her.

She fears
it might slice
her open, tear her
to thin shrieks.

At the Door

A splinter in the paw,
the wolf stops its stalk,
its scratch at the window,
lies down in the snow,
snuffles and nips.

In the quiet before
the cloudy mirror,
she braids her
long gray locks,
caresses her once
soft face, fingers
carved dry lines.
Meager soup
on the fire, watery
lentils and the last
bone of the lamb.

So empty—she
is tempted to open
the door, call in
the wolf. If he will
let her, she will urge
him to lie down
on the hearth, she will
pull out his thorn,
she will stretch out
beside him. Perhaps
she is almost ready—
if he eats her, better
than this long slow
loneliness. A few quick
bites, the flow of blood
to show she has been alive.

She would be somebody's
meal, somebody's
satisfaction.

Sloppy Woman

A sloppy woman takes up space softly,
her rugs fuzzy with dust and un-brushed dog,
sheets silkened with skin oils and lazy scent.
Her great gingham skirt hides buttocks like feathers,
thick fur that curls around her satin slit.

You should be so lucky to find such a woman.
Rich smells spill from her oily hair,
the creases in front of her elbows,
her fingers and toes. If you touch her,
pretty man, she will make a soup
of ancient secrets. She will put you in
and stir you up. She will witch you good.

Women Writing

A crystal hangs
in the window,
forms a prism
through which to view
the greenery beyond.
A rainbow collects
in its tiny fist.
There is tarragon
in the garden,
a sweet green burn
on the tongue.
A shaggy cat,
of course, curled
at the door,
neither in nor out.
There are women
alive in beauty
gathered tight
in their hard bones,
making poems
from their scrap piles,
chained sparrow,
lost bread,
brilliant beads.

Thalia

From the gloom
at stage edge,
a flash of flesh,
the sudden bright slash
of fierce face as Thalia begins
to remove her regalia.
She twirls her pink
parasol, throws it to the side.
Her mass of red hair
falls forward as she
leans to slip garters
from her long legs,
slides the maddening
black stockings down
one by one, tosses them
toward the whistles and hoots
in the front row. She turns
her back on their avidity.
Gas light hisses. It feels
so good to be bad. Thalia
releases the laces
on her corset, turns to reveal
a coy freckled bosom,
teases off her lacy white
bloomers slow, slow
as silk. Right hand on
right hip, red bush blazing,
she gives them one good
look, glides off the stage.

Maud

In the womb
her tiny fingers
felt the tiny fingers
of her sister,
the toes of her feet
probed a face,
learned a nose,
a mouth, a pair
of ears. The girls
circled each other
in a tight dance
of recognition,
of identical
otherness. Then
emerging from
the sweetness
of satiation,
from the soup
where every need
was met and shared,
Maud came alone
to light and air,
her sister lost
at the gate
to the world.
For eighty-six years
a wound
Maud couldn't close.

On Isabel's Big Island

The night relief arrives. We are guiltily glad to retreat
from our stepmother's house to the five tidy acres,
comfort, of the house we have rented

for the week, to a beer and sandwich on the lanai,
to an early night, sound sleep interrupted by
the brief violent beat of rain.

Daytimes, Isabel is lifted onto her recliner, turned
away from her gardenias, pink hibiscus,
yellow roses slowly succumbing to weeds and rot.

These are the days of Hilo's Merri Monarch
Festival—dancers from all of Polynesia
gathered here in competition. The TV is on

but Isabel's eyes are closed. This time she doesn't
have the strength to care who loses or wins. Sometimes
she is sufficiently at ease to doze and snore.

She moans in distress. Her hand lifts to signal yes.
My brother places her on her potty chair. I wipe her
and wash her, and once she is resettled in her chaise,

I massage her feet. Her glance is still fierce. She hates
our seeing her like this, unable to speak, to stand,
to move anything but her feeble hands and toes.

Day and night get equal time in Hawaii, dark comes
down at six, lifts at six. On the lanai, papaya for breakfast.
Rain sluices off the roof into the black lava-lined pond.

Fish scatter, seek shelter beneath fat fleshy green
water hyacinth. Then the spigot turns, rain stops,
steam rises from rich growth spread thin

over black lava crumbles. A rat darts from
his miniature lava cave, makes a pink and brown
dash to the dog's dish, steals a water-logged Kibble.

After our father died, Isabel, fifth generation Vermonter,
found refuge in Pahoa, interest in Hawaii's violent life
of fire, steam, ever-spreading molten rolls and spikes.

Unlike the first Yankees who came here, she was neither
proselytizer nor entrepreneur—her only interest to see
and learn something dramatic, new, feel the warmth.

Now dead insects, thick dust, coat her windowsills. Streaks
of mildew, pits of rust, stain the once white surface of
her refrigerator still full, as are the cabinets and freezer,

of food she cannot eat. She is fed by a tube inserted
through her stomach wall. A pillow on the sofa
is embroidered "A book lover never goes to bed alone,"

and bookcase after bookcase of abandoned mysteries
attest to that now lost love. We leave early today.
At the market, red flowers of the ohia-lehua tree

brush a tin roof. Beneath, women hawk, for five dollars,
red ginger, bird of paradise, anthurium in great clusters.
They offer little apple bananas, papaya, mango, and one

particularly un-beguiling fruit, rambutan, spiny like
a red sea urchin. A vendor demonstrates for us, splits it,
bites white sweet flesh away from the brown seed.

Back at our rental we walk among orange hibiscus,
purple and white orchids, baby pineapples in a circle
of leaf spikes. Ripe oranges thud. Giant lemons fall.

A scurry of geckos in unlikely colors, peach, neon-green—
then—coqui, coqui—the song of imported tree frogs overwhelms
the night. Another violent shower beats on the roof, stops dead.

All we can do is sign some papers, make some calls,
encourage the care-givers who are already doing so much.
Too late for cure or pleasure—too late to give Isabel one more

glimpse of Madame Pele's power, her never-ending fire,
her slow slide that buries houses, roads, until she tumbles
at last hissing into the sea, groaning out new land.

"No parents, cancer, moonlight through the window"

poetry guidelines from an unnamed press

Well, then, is the postmistress
acceptable, the one who lived
to be one hundred and four
despite the dusty window,
the almost empty town,
tumbleweed the only thing
beating at her door?

Occasional lizards skittered
past as she rocked on cracked
dry wood. With tired ears
she listened for the car
of relatives who brought
food, left before she could
begin her story one more time.

Buildings split and flaked
in desert wind, screens sagged,
cottonwoods spilled yellow leaves
onto the arroyo's crusted dirt.
She thought there once had been
wild currants and gooseberries. When
had this become a desiccated place?
She couldn't remember.

Flashes

A flash in the corner of her eye—
the pair of chickadees is back,
in and out the round door
of their old birdhouse. Windows
closed against a spring storm
are closed against frantic calls,
lusty songs. In this empty house
there is only one silence against
another. She watches hail strip
new blossoms from gray branches,
rain barrels overflow with water
and ice, bright daffodils flatten
in thick mud. A beaver, the first
in years, has been seen downtown,
just west of the Camino Alire Bridge.
He doesn't know the river water is
intermittent, the flow controlled
by engineers at the Reservoir,
his home soon to be a mound
of dust. Against these eager lives,
measured in minutes, hours, days,
hers suddenly feels endless.

Triolet

A backward somersault into the night,

While all these years she has planned to begin.

Day after day relinquished without a fight,

Her backward somersault into the night.

Domestic duty, naps, breaking news, some political fight,

Until evening smiles its ironic grin.

A backward somersault into the night,

While all these years she has planned to begin.

Complete

The moon's
long shine,
slap of water
against shadowed
dock, soft silk
of black waves
brushing bare skin.
Floating alone
beneath glitter sky,
long-tressed
water weeds
caress her back.
Eyes closed,
drifting
into forever.

Prayer

Let the boy cherish his goat
      and his sister.

Let crickets sing
      in watered fields.

Let naked women be naked
      by choice.

Let streams fill,
      clear and cold.

Let angry old men retire
      to drink scotch,
      mumble in leather chairs.

Let the stars point the way
      to unimaginable galaxies.

Let her sheets be clean,
      a hand gently touch her face.

III

Lost Stories

There are many mysteries in this house.
Who made, who owned, who sold,
who shipped this faded coffer of black lacquer?

Who is the gilt god? Why does the monkey
offer it his half-eaten banana? What does
the elephant proffer in the sealed vessel
held high in its curling trunk?

And these Japanese ladies portrayed
in colored stones, gossiping in their pagodas,
walking gracefully on lacquer paths,
being poled across a pond between
lotus blossoms and a pair of loving ducks?
The story was clear to someone, its flowers
of magnolia, pear, the peony and the raspberry,
the tall green shrub.

That chest, pale wood clean, scrubbed,
sent across the world, sags with age.
How many times have its fifty-five drawers
been emptied and filled with cures, clothes,
silks, laces, seeds, envelopes from forgotten
or forgiven lovers, memories of generations
now gone? Once upon a time a tiny worm
curled back to its origins, carved a letter
in its own alphabet, and so lives on and on.

Year's End

Outside the world is slowed and hushed
under the season's first real snowfall.

Inside, time presses, a millennia
of winters, short, dark days.

A rush of memory—lost ones gather
around a table, confront life-long lines
of pumpkin pie, roasted turkeys, successions
of scraggily fir trees, tangled strings of lights.

The odor of supper cooking spreads
into every cold corner, down every dark hallway,
mingles with the sound of piano scales,
frigid blast from an opening door,
the stamp of snowy feet.

A candle on the windowsill melting frost
forms a small circle of light.

A brother, a sister, dispensed to individual
icy sheets, wishing the family could squeeze
together into one warm bed.

"Moving toward infinity in these meandering and transient, minute details"

Raoul Dufy

Twin rings of yellow mist
around the streetlight and the moon

Cats, soft, warm, loved, who
disappear anyway

Names and days that slip away—
a raft floundering in a cold gray sea

Pale cheese hardening on a board,
the paring knife's darkened blade,
splitting handle

Her mother's kitchen,
polished maple counters,
a green stove on legs

An ordinary family buttering toast

January

Awkward on old crust, again and again
Caesar's hind legs give way. He looks back at me,
but eager to lead, he struggles up.
It may be easier where the deer's pointed weight
has churned the surface. I urge him
onto that trail, past holes melted by spoor,
like buckshot through a road sign,
past chewed ends of twigs. The large prints
that wander off alone are those of a buck,
this scrabbled trail through the snow
picked out by does and fawns. The gallantry
of deer and dogs, I suppose, a matter of instinct.

From my window snow has the dull sheen
of old silver beneath feathered clouds, gray arrows
edged with purple. Yesterday, when the cardinal
flew against the window, gray feathers from his breast
scattered. Only the tips were red. I would never
have guessed the bird without seeing the body.

The regular rhythm of Mother's morning bath
was the last thing she gave up.

Sestina I

Mother was a breakfast saint, oatmeal, juice,
homemade bread toasted, scrambled eggs on a plate,
while we listened to the radio, distant wobbling wave
after wave of war news, a correspondent's leaking vase
of air strikes, advances, retreats in heat or snow,
assurances we were on victory's inexorable road.

Then we each went out on our day's road,
fortified by our time around the table, juiced
up, ready for Vermont's furious winter, ice and snow,
the lake frozen partly in swells, partly into a frozen plate.
Our lives were stalks of bittersweet in a sturdy vase
before the end of a gray-brown war released a new wave

of color. At each school-day's end, released too, glad to wave
good-bye to fellow prisoners, we set off on the road
home through falling flakes, the world an upside-down vase,
everything hidden in blizzard thick as a pour of juice
that quick-stopped. Then low sun shimmered like silver-plate.
Snow-suited slogs up and up, delirious sled ride down new snow.

No matter where I've since lived, fresh snow
has brought the tug of memory in long rolling waves—
every evening setting the table with glasses and plates
as wool snowsuits hung odiferous on the radiators. From the road,
sounds of chains splashing slush turned to iced juice
by salt. Inside, on the buffet, dried silver-dollars in a vase.

In my home too I've tried never to leave a vase
empty, something dried when the ground is snow-
covered. Mother grew poppies like bright orange juice.
First, daffodils, iris and bleeding heart gave way to waves
of peonies, yellow roses, daphne, proceeding down the road
of their natural order as the world slides slow on its tectonic plates.

51

The garden comes to mind whenever I see flowery china plates,
fine porcelain. Mother used Father's precious vases,
his dragon platters, to contain her flowers, serve our food. The road
from Father's teaching days in China a long one, gone like snow.
As for his accumulated treasures, he was not ready to wave
good-by to them—his pitcher only for serving company exotic juice.

Mother did not believe in holding back juice glasses or pretty plates.
She waved hello to useful things, put flowers in his favorite vase.
Hair turned to snow, but still the two mostly happy down their road.

Lake Champlain

Like lake sand
yesterday washes in and out—
closer than tomorrow.

The view from the shore is too wide.
I'll turn my back on it.

The faded red cabin
resting on gray rock, the reflection
of fir trees on dark water.

Are they true?

Or only anchors I imagined
to steady my mind.

Lakeview

The moss has nearly obliterated the names
on the modest little gravestones. We couldn't
find them at first, had to study the lake,
then the sloping hillside, remember where
the graves lay in relation to the ferry slip,
the harbor restaurant down below.
We brought brushes and bleach,
but they didn't do much to clear away
gray-green growth of lichen, black mold.
Mother would be disappointed to discover
how casual we have been about upkeep.
Grandmother would tell us not to trouble
ourselves. Father would be happy about
improvements to the harbor, the new museum,
would suggest the stones might last longer
if they were better cared for. Grandfather
would hope we might say a prayer, but
with voices kept low so as not to draw
attention, make spectacles of ourselves.

I've suggested my ashes be scattered
surreptitiously there on the green lawn,
around the scraggily hydrangea we planted
so long ago. I would like to know
the lake was close at hand, that we were
together once again, as though we were
picnicking in the yard on Cliff Street,
Grandfather's garden beans and lettuce
fixed in a salad, Mother's orange poppies
on the table, all of us finishing quickly
before fireflies lit the gathering dark,
before the mosquitoes came to plague us.

Ghazal in Black, White and Gray

Blown sideways in winter's frigid throe,
a flock of bushtits like drops of snow.

As the sun lights a solstice path,
Yule fires burn, melting the old year's snow.

Gray velvet feathers, rising cranes, leave
the gray still pond to settle on fields of snow.

On black lacquer, a raging lion and a furious horse
carved in ivory and mother-of-pearl white as snow.

One with a dove, one with a lute, one with a horn,
three white clay angels like hardened snow.

Vowels, God's breath, hovering over, under, through
the black on white of the Torah, ink on snow.

Her songs: Edith's daughter sings melodies
dark of night, gray of sleet, flash of snow.

IV

The October Patio

I
The old dog licks
the bloody spot
on his left hind leg,
rests his long head
over his left forepaw,
twitches twice.

II
Grass swells
with fine rain.
Water collects
in a white pitcher
on the picnic table.
Lilac leaves fold
into themselves.

III
Maple leaves blow
sideways. So many
remain, this detachment
makes no apparent
difference. Only
the black walnut
is bare. Dark
branches,
delicate
veins and nerves
against gray sky.

Russian Olive

Unwelcome immigrant, waste tree, water grabber,
two years ago we could have uprooted you,
tossed you down the draw, used you for erosion control,

but now you are twelve feet of narrow trunk. Your roots
stretch to sources of water we knew nothing about
while all around native trees struggle.

Your bark is smooth as tanned deerskin, burgundy branches
barbed-wire studded with green thorns, bristled with beige buds.
A few oval olives linger like cinnamon drops

crusted hard. Dusty flesh clings to dark pits
even the birds don't bother. Sudden sun shimmers you,
silhouetted against white-clouded winter sky.

Obdurate, you sway with the winter winds.
We wouldn't wish to cut you down now. Despite
your unruly ways, we'll leave you to make your own luck.

Night Whorls

Splinter in the eye

Splash of scarlet

Bone in the begging bowl

Black song

Long whispering wrapped in green velvet

Scent of silk

Twist the tiger's tail until the dream lets go

Pieces of jigsaw whirl in the wind

She buries her poems behind the wall

Awake she is open, empty and lost

The Sound Cure

Waking early once again, she slips outside.
Wrapped in her winter bathrobe she sits
in a sheltered corner. In the dark a wet wind
stirs heavy pines.

One round tone rings from the large wind chime,
then a cluster of deep notes. An answering flurry,
an icy skitter, a splinter of high sharp sounds from
the little chime that hangs beside it.

Now and then a drip of melt splashes
onto the frozen water of the rain barrels,
murmur of a voice across the arroyo, distant
susurration of car tires, far-off whistle of a train.

Every window of the man's house at the top
of the hill is ablaze with light, as it is every night.
Does he have trouble sleeping too? Maybe she
should tell him to try her sound cure,
to step out to the whisper of dry grass fronds,
gentle fall of snow from invisible branches.

In Willow Month

Tiny, tinny streams of water drip, business-like,
steady, from the roof.

The delicate *raow, raow* of the calico cat
as it arches against a hand.
April sun has turned its fur to soft fire.

In ancient Rome on this day
before a cheering crowd
foxes were released,
burning sticks fixed to their tails,
a ritual meant to protect
the year's crop from disease.

Here a beetle explores five
pale petals of pasqueflower,
the yellow spikes of its open heart,
while outside the bloom, a hairless bee,
striped in bold yellow and black, faintly buzzes
impatient interest in stamen and stigma.

Yesterday, after the blue jay
ate their last fledgling, the finches,
ferrying bits of grass one after the other,
were busy repairing their plundered nest.

Watch

Hissing insinuation,
warning rattle beneath
an impenetrable
thicket of wild roses,
crenellation of leaves,
single pink blooms
scattered on prickled stems.

Big burgundy ants
emerge from nests
of shifted sand,
sifted stones, to bite
a careless ankle.
The ants unpack
tight clay, release rock,
alter the landscape
one grain at a time.

All year the beauty bush
sheds strips of gray bark
from tangled limbs,
prepares for its one glory—
tiny trumpets, palest pink,
lined with a lace tracery of orange,
ethereal white anther and pistil,
a bounty, open, gone.

I've had longer to go
and come. Again this year
I can regret how fast
the Scotch Broom's
medicinal scent,
yellow flowers are
fading. Myself, a weathered

perennial drooping blooms,
apparently still has some
seasons to observe and record.

And what do they matter—
a few blossoms, an ant,
a snake, a rose—an excuse
for letting hours, days,
months, years drift by?

A haphazard record of a lucky life—
I hope you won't mind if I bring
these small things to your attention.

A Young Buck—

browses his way through the yard,
his antlers still encased in velvet,
his young balls bobbing. We look
at each other through the window.
One of his large ears bends toward
me, then the other. He resumes
his meditative munching, moves
slowly down the slope of the draw.
Politely, he ignores the flower beds,
the May-fresh shrubbery, for the wild
flowers, wild food he knows best.
He is welcome anytime.

At the Wheel of the Year

The leg scratch of crickets sounds
from drying sage. Thunder rolls
from white clouds out of the west.
Wind on her summer-burnt arms
is a soft stroking, neither warm nor cool.
This is the time of the singing moon.

One angry skrank of a jay.
In uncharacteristic silence,
a chickadee eats seed. Day-lily
leaves yellow, dry seed stalks
rattle, burrs wait for the unwary.

Orange butterflies have curled their tongues
back from rich purple blossoms of buddleia,
sit on pink sandstone, open and close their wings—
Satiation? Thanksgiving? Farewell? They rest.
At a signal in butterfly they rise together
into the breeze, beat their way back
to their purple banquet.

All around is abundance, bloom, seed,
sun and breeze, cloud and sky,
mountain and green meadow,
orange zinnia, purple aster, yellow goldenrod.
Larvae wriggle in the watery hollow of a rock.
The world does sing, then holds its breath
in the final moment before the cold comes down.

Matter

Once water flowed
on Mars, perhaps does now
deep beneath
its cold red surface.
Surrounding
its matter, all matter, us,
dark energy's tiny tug.
This infinitesimal darkness,
unfelt, unseen,
links everything,
spreads, shapes
all we know,
more than we can
imagine.

Here on what feels
like solid ground
she grows
a garden of rocks.
A miniature
wasteland
holds flecks,
gleams of light,
a gray web of tiny worm tracks,
a pool of crystal,
a meandering river
of yellow algae,
clusters like black pearls
frozen in black stone—
fractured pieces
of a larger whole.
From the world's
skeleton, she arranges
fragments of its bones.

Pilgrimage—the Tarot of Ketuah, the Spice Woman

It is time. Crystals pour from a ruby pitcher
while flames rise painlessly from each
cupped palm. Abraham's third wife
sings a song of memory, one more good-bye.
She carries spices through the parched desert,
gives each welcome oasis the name of the child
she bears there, and in gratitude for restoring waters,
bequeaths something from her bundles of destiny
and obligation. Beneath black skies, bright skies,
against choking sting of sand, she continues
her journey. Carrying her fate with her, she finds her way.

Say the Same Things

about seeds
about winter and spring
about beginning
        at the end
about the long slow middle
that seems to go nowhere

about the ice jam in the canale
the baby cones of the piñon,
the greed of gray jays,

say the same things about
blue—skies and eyes,

but honor the strange, the scaly spikes
of iguanas, lurid green purple,
their scrabbling toes,
patient wait for things we don't notice

honor the gophers who
win, the crystal drop of water
that casts back the world, the new
hollyhock leaf,
a baby's thumbnail

and red, thimble berries
like colored glass, strawberries
in a long green row, her satin dress

honor the phone call, the voice
of a friend who has no bad news
or the one who does

Two Layers of Clouds Blow

in opposite directions,
the lower in wisps like
milkweed down, the upper
in a jolly collection
of giants' beards. Two
forces in opposition,
obeying contrary rules,
in harmony with some
stronger impulse, some
universal law of wind
and air. Although the two
do not travel together,
still they share the mystery
of contrary movement.

Sestina II

There are many ways to exit the shadow
of her days. She could fold it like paper, crinkle
it in a ball of silver foil, paint
it the colors she likes best, the red sleeve
that holds her imaginary arrows, blue sky that touches
everything, yellow of coreopsis, chamisa, other landscape litter.

Once, beneath the old furnace's giant boiler, a litter
of kittens. Their mother tucked them into the dirt, mere shadows,
tiny mews, blind eyes, fragile struggle of paws. Touched,
the girl considered their faces, crinkled
like Christmas paper. She lay a kitten on her sleeve,
examined its random calico, like splotches of paint.

Silhouetted against red sandstone mountains, paint
ponies move slowly over sparse grass, lay down in dry litter.
A canyon trail passes little caves pieced in like sleeves,
perhaps formed by the rub and tumble of rocky creek. Shadows
slip slow across the narrow space, reveal folds and crinkles
of stone. After the hard descent, water's welcome touch.

Nature's fat stew, hard beauty, appeal to her. The touch
of human drive often squandered in strut. Man may paint
over the striving, call it glory—discoveries a puny crinkle
in creation. Now, she thinks, we have ventured out, litter
space with leftover junk, little mistakes. Our remnants shadow
earth's spin. The cosmos still holds vast surprises up its sleeve.

Tonight she wonders if something massive will be un-sleeved
while she still lives, a super volcano, the fearsome touch
of an asteroid that spreads fire and dirt to shadow
the earth. Its awesome chokehold may well paint
most everything out of the picture; remains, so much litter
from which new life will emerge, small crinkles

in the universe where massive explosions, dust clouds, crinkle
space. From the edge of time, through dark matter's sleeve,
where star nurseries, star creations and extinctions litter
and shoot out bits and chunks of matter that falling, touch,
spawn minerals, molecules, that form and paint
everything she knows, colors she loves, star dust to final shadow.

She is glad to exist in the shadow and crinkle of time
whose pressure paints her days like a rainbow sleeve
of silk; its touch urges her to ignore life's everyday litter.

Living on Earth

Desperate for a drink
       this dry winter,
an unlikely amalgam of birds
       clusters on the birdbath's rim.
A flicker pecks briskly
       at frozen water. The black grin
of feathers across his chest
       disappears and reappears
as his head bends and lifts,
       bends and lifts.
The other birds are wary of his bill.
       House finches and towhees,
juncos and sparrows,
       even a bright goldfinch,
wait their chance, do not fly away.

They say the ever-expanding universe
       burst out
of a marble-sized bit of matter
       in a trillion trillionth of a second.
From that unimaginable moment
       to this rich speck
of struggling abundance—
       what are the impossible odds
that I should be here as witness?

Elizabeth Raby has been a poet in the schools for the Pennsylvania Council of the Arts, the New Jersey Council of the Arts, and the Geraldine R. Dodge Foundation. She taught poetry writing at Muhlenberg College. She earned a B.A. in History from Vassar College, an M.A. in English (Creative Writing) from Temple University, and is a fellow of the Virginia Center for the Creative Arts. In the summers of 2006 and 2007, Ms. Raby represented the Teachers for Tomorrow program as an English teacher in Deva, Romania. Elizabeth, Patricia Goodrich, and Casandra Ioan collaborated on a bi-lingual poetry collection, *Bone, Flesh & Fur or Oase, Carne & Blană*. The poems were translated by Ms. Ioan and published by Petoskey Stone Press. Ms. Raby's other publications include *The Year the Pears Bloomed Twice*, Virtual Artists Collective; *The Hard Scent of Peonies*, Jasper Press; *Camphorwood*, Nightshade Press; and *Ten Degrees Above Zero*, Jasper Press. She lives in Santa Fe, New Mexico.

Breinigsville, PA USA
28 January 2010
231560BV00002B/4/P